Unmute

Monologues For Young People, By Young People

Salamander Street

First published in 2022 by Salamander Street Ltd., a Wordville imprint.
(info@salamanderstreetcom).

PB ISBN: 9781914228827

10 9 8 7 6 5 4 3 2 1

Cover artwork by India Buxton

Further copies of this publication can be purchased from
www.salamanderstreet.com.

All profits from this book will go towards future projects with young
people.

Wordville

Acknowledgements

With thanks to our *Unmute* readers: Millie Bloom, Edith Keays, Camille Koosyial, Sally Macalister, Lowri Matias and Trudy Siskind-Weiss. And our *Unmute* performers: Massimiliano Acerbi, Bianca Bewley, Sydney Crocker, Danni Davis, Jesse Dunbar, Andy Jenks, Noah Lukehurst, Morag Massey, Jack Price, Che Tligui.

A heartfelt thank you to the youth workers, teachers, youth theatre directors and artists who carved out the time and space to get young people writing. This anthology wouldn't have been possible without you.

Finally, a big thank you to all the young people who took part in *Unmute*. Each and every one of you has a powerful, special and inspiring voice. Now more than ever, the world needs good writers. Keep writing!

About Us

Bristol Old Vic Theatre School

Bristol Old Vic Theatre School is one of the most successful and well- respected conservatoire drama schools in the UK. We attract the very best talent in students and staff, and our courses are recognised nationally and internationally as a benchmark of quality in professional acting, technical, production and management training.

www.oldvic.ac.uk

@BOVTS

LUNG

Founded in Barnsley in 2014, LUNG is a campaign-led arts charity, working UK wide to make hidden voices heard. We are company in residence with the National Theatre and partners with The Lowry in Salford.

Our work takes multiple forms:

- We develop high quality verbatim productions that tour from theatres to school halls to the Houses of Parliament
- We create educational and training resources for teachers, social workers and people in power
- We spearhead award winning campaigns to spark change

Our plays are published by Faber & Faber and studied on the AQA GCSE Drama Syllabus. We believe in the value of art to amplify untold stories and its power to transform the world around us.

www.lungtheatre.co.uk

@lungtheatre

Salamander Street

Salamander Street is an independent publisher, founded in Leith, Edinburgh in 2019 by George Spender. In 2023, it was acquired by performing arts press Wordville. We publish books about the performing arts including plays, non-fiction, poetry and educational resources.

www.salamanderstreet.com

@salamanderst

Foreword

A teacher called us in the middle of the pandemic to tell us about a student they were working with. This student wanted to perform a monologue they'd written for their drama GCSE. It was about mental health. About their own mental health. The student was struggling and their drama class was a space they felt they could express themselves, open up a conversation and perhaps begin to understand what they were going through.

When the senior leadership team at this school learnt about the monologue, they said it could not be performed because it explored challenging themes. This student would have only been performing this monologue to their teacher and a camera. But still, the school said no. The student wasn't allowed to do it.

This teacher called us to ask for our advice on censorship. They'd created a space where young people felt able to be open, honest, authentic. And then that space had been taken away.

LUNG is a campaign-led verbatim theatre company. This means the words that people say form the scripts that we make. In our work with young people we are often exploring the theme of censorship. How do you allow young people to genuinely explore their voice and have agency over the stories they want to tell, if they are making work within structures that have so many rules and regulations?

That phone call with a teacher ignited something. What would happen if we created a platform for young people across the UK to say whatever they wanted? And what would happen if the only parameter we set was: 'Do you feel like sometimes your voice isn't heard? And if so, what message do you want to share with the world?'

Unmute is the product of that ignition. On the journey of pulling this anthology together we've had conversations with young people from across the UK – time and again the themes that have come up are voice and censorship. A lot of the time, grownups say that they want to hear from young people. But do they really?

Theatre is a space for tackling challenging and uncomfortable subjects. In the wake of a pandemic and in the face of so much upheaval and uncertainty we need to amplify the authentic voices of young people, now more than ever. We need to hear young voices that challenge, young voices that provoke, young voices that disrupt. Hear these voices. Then act upon what they have to say.

Helen Monks and Matt Woodhead

Co-Directors, LUNG

Top Tips For Performing a Monologue

This book is packed with brilliant monologues; there are vivid characters, unique voices and insightful things being said. These monologues are waiting for you to bring them to life and that means inhabiting the characters with authenticity (imagine yourself as the character, with their life experiences) and lifting the words off the page so it feels thought and spoken rather than just read out loud. Try these tips to help:

Who is your character speaking to?
Are you speaking to a group of people, or just one person? Are you speaking to a friend? Or an enemy? Or someone you've not seen in a long time?

Where are you?
Are you in a public space (like the park or the shops) or a private space (like in someone's house?) Might people overhear you and does that matter?

What are you trying to achieve?
Why are you telling someone this story? For example, are you trying to share a secret or guilt trip them into something? Perhaps you are trying to confide in a friend.

How do you want to affect the person you are speaking to?
Do you want them to do something or feel a certain way?

When are the turning points in the speech?
Do you change your mind or change tactics to get what you want? Make the thoughts fresh as if they are coming to you in the moment.

Do you change during the speech?
Are you different at the end of the monologue to the person you were at the beginning?

Good luck with using these monologues and who knows; I may even hear some of them in auditions for Bristol Old Vic Theatre School.

Jenny Stephens, Artistic Director

Bristol Old Vic Theatre School

Contents

Some of the monologues in this volume contain
strong language and content that some readers
might find distressing including the subjects of
racism, suicide, disordered eating
and coercive control.

The Battle of a Teenage Pole Vaulter

Charis Crawford

CHARIS: The official calls my name. 'Stand at 50 please.' The ritual begins. My dance and my mantra. Then my body which is almost always in motion… is still. The pole into position at my waist. Breathe. Rock. Push all the thoughts out with a song in my head but they keep popping back.

What's for dinner tonight? Why do the words jumble up on the page? I wonder what time F1 qualifying is? Why did he do it?

Start to run. Counting my steps. One. Two.

Maybe it's chicken noodle soup.

Three. Four.

See my world through a blue reading overlay.

Five. Six. Seven. Eight.

Maybe Leclerc will again.

One. Two. Three.

Could I have made my uncle change his mind?

The runway is my race track. Focus in on the goal. Plant the pole. It's a distinct sound - the pole hitting the box. Impact.

A hurricane of thoughts. Ice cream for pudding? Who…how…are… our… the spellings all get muddled. Ferrari for pole position. I want my Uncle back.

I swing up as the bar is looming. Propel into the air. There's no other feeling like this. Push away the pole. My support is gone.

Dinner… Dyslexia… Ferrari… Suicide… swirling in my head. Flight, and a moment of silence. The bar is wobbling beneath me.

Boom. Hit the mat. Eyes locked on the bar. It stays and I smile. I have battled with the bar and my pole and I have won. For two seconds I have silenced the thoughts. Run away from reality. I'm free.

Time to do it again. But higher.

Unmute

Farah Farooq

SURVIVOR: People talk constantly, buzzing about their lives, like pretty little bees, not noticing seeds wilting in the background while they tend to their flowers.

MUTE.

Nobody really likes the silence anymore, they try desperately to cover it because, back then that's all we heard.

REWIND.

I was 13 when it started, when the world ended. Now I'll be 16 this year. So much for the 'best years of my life'.

PAUSE.

I remember the day when I first heard about it. The pandemic. Don't be scared, it's not a taboo word, not anymore. It seemed like a thing out of a history book, so far away, barely touching me yet coming closer still.

FAST FORWARD.

Now nobody cares anymore. It's all gone. All the people in the world forgetting the horrors of which we have endured. Because they want to forget.

PAUSE.

Don't forget. Ever. Don't forget the people who died. Don't forget the people who survived and never forget the tears you cried. Don't forget the wilting seeds, don't spend time on the blooming flowers when they are temporary. Don't be a busy little bee.

UNMUTE.

Let us hear your voice and let you never forget.

PLAY.

She Doesn't Even Care

Dantey Dean

LEO: Miss! Miss! Miss! It's no use, she never listens to me. She never even notices I'm here. It's like not fair.

(To the person next to them.) You want a pencil? Yeah sure.

Basically what I was saying is like she doesn't pay attention to me. She'll listen to you, you're a boy, you're important. But me, the quiet girl at the back of the class, she doesn't even notice when I'm asking for help. Like waving my…

(To the person next to them.) You want a pen? Here, take my whole pencil case.

Anyway, the point is, she'll pay attention to people who are not me. People who don't have a pen or a pencil.

(To the person next to them.) What? You want my chair? Where did your chair go?

Like look at me, I have to stand here and do my work stood up, and yet she still hasn't noticed. Look at me sacrificing my pens, my pencils, even my blooming chair for people who don't even care about this lesson. And I'm stood here trying to figure it out. It looks like a bunch of scribbles on the paper.

(To the teacher.) Oh hi Miss, yeah, thanks, no, I don't really need that much help, you can go and help someone else.

See she doesn't even care.

That Uncontrollable Tic,Tic,Tic

Beth Noble

GEORGINA: It started just under a year ago. I don't know why. But that is when I lost control. It started slow. The occasional twitch, a flinch. It got worse.

My head would flick, so would my limbs. I just can't control it! I am a risk not just to myself but others too. No one understands the feeling. That cold shudder before you tic, tic, tic.

Most people understand and just back away so I don't hurt them. It makes you feel so alone unless you know others like you. But then some people insult and laugh!

Why don't they understand?! I just can't control the tic, tic, ticing.

I hide it at school. It looks strange, abnormal. It feels like you're being possessed by some evil demon. You just can't control it.

There is NO control over the tic, tic, ticing. Except during sleep. The peace and quiet and stillness is refreshing. But then you wake again for another day of uncontrollable tic, tic, ticing.

If I concentrate on something it stops, but it always returns. You try to fight the relentless demon, attempting to suppress it. But it never lasts. Then the tic, tic, ticing begins again and you just lose control. It feels good to release the demon and be myself but, sometimes…

The tic, tic, ticing just makes you want to break down and cry! I will hold back the tears and hide the tic, tic, ticing. Until…

People understand and accept the tic, tic, ticing as something that just happens. And the insulting silences.

And it becomes quiet and the world is peaceful and accepting towards those that have the uncontrollable tic, tic, tic.

Dave Doesn't Like It When You Say 'No'

Jessica Humphreys

JESSICA: I met Dave through a group of friends. At first, Dave seemed so nice and caring. Dave woke me up with such nice messages. Dave complimented me, shored up the foundations of my rickety self-esteem. Opened the door to self-worth and let me glimpse potential happiness.

He said he loved me.

I said 'I love you too, Dave', but after a few days of us being together he decided he 'got too comfortable.'

It started off with minor things like little digs dressed up as 'banter'. The sort that seems friendly enough at first glance, but look a little closer and you see they are designed to keep you off balance - to not become too happy that you might feel confident enough to go it alone. I dealt with it. It was water off a duck's back, I told myself, because it felt good knowing somebody loved me.

Words designed to control, turned to physical acts. Then it got worse. You see, Dave doesn't like it when you say 'no'.

A few weeks ago, we went to the park, it was peaceful. We sat on a bench and watched the swans. He tried to force me into doing… things with him but I said 'I don't want to'. We were in public. I was not brought up that way. Dave does not like it when you say 'no'.

The next day he saw I was upset, but didn't ask about the bruises which he must've known were beginning to bloom beneath my cute dress which he likes me to wear. He took me on a date to the cinema. On the back row, where the lovers sit, he touched me again. I must have pulled a face or said the wrong thing because Dave was not happy. Dave does not like it when you say 'no' even if you don't say the word 'no'.

I got the silent treatment until no one else was there to see and hear what Dave had to say on the matter. Dave spent a lot of money. Dave went to all that effort. I was ungrateful. Why did I not love him back? Why could I not show him that I love him too?

I posted the pictures of the bruises Dave had given me and it started going viral. Dave couldn't handle it. Whilst I was in the police station he took my pills from my bedside table.

His funeral is next week. I don't think many people will go.

Dave didn't like it when you said 'no'.

Hair

Sophia Beadle

SHAKUN *is a teenage girl of British South Asian heritage, leaning very close to a mirror, plucking her eyebrows*

SHAKUN: Hair… lots of it… everywhere. Y'know I sometimes look at myself in the mirror digging for this excruciatingly deep and excruciatingly dark hair between my eyebrows and think for a second, surely I'm actually meant to leave it there? It's not doing anything wrong. What am I even doing it for? It's not like I look forward to a nightly ritual of letting out all my anger on a poor eyebrow hair for an hour… pfft. *(Shrugs, resumes plucking.)* It's just a passing thought. Oh come on… ow! Lose focus for one second and cut myself, ugh… I've got some concealer, it's not exactly my skin tone but it's the best Boots could do.

I've had the burden of not just being a little brown girl in a white town but a very confident one too. When people already see you as a bit different you wouldn't dare take one step away from the standard all the white girls live up to… Oh and I know they have their insecurities, we all do. It's funny, everyone is secretly united by the fact we all have insecurities about things we can't help, yet we still impose them onto each other by subconsciously judging everyone all the time. At least it would be nice to fit in as easily as those white girls. They're so pretty, you can't help but zone out wishing you looked like that.

It's fine though, you get used to it, like, I've been getting my face waxed since I was 11. *(Suddenly checks her face.)* Hmm… *(Grabs a razor and uses it on her upper lip.)* One time I almost forgot my mum's name because I refused to tell it to anyone for so long, and I stopped asking for leftovers in my packed lunches ages ago. I'm not embarrassed… I love my mum, it's just a… compromise. Plus, her food is actually amazing – you should taste her rendang – I just eat it at home, where I can use my hands without the dirty looks. Oh, she understands the struggle anyway, she got her eyebrows thinned 20 years ago…

(Suddenly serious.) After 2001… I guess the need to appear more… Eurocentric… became apparent. It's really fucking annoying having

to go through an hour of extra airport security with strip searches, or being stopped at the entrance of a shopping centre to get your bags checked. It's disgusting enough that people are wary of Muslims but when I remember she has a crucifix around her neck at all times… that treatment really does come down to skin sometimes.

Beat.

Anyway, it's not like I can just hide who I am. I was going to wear a lehenga to prom until I found out you can't really get one fitted here. *(Smiles.)* I would've looked so pretty.

(Laughs.) I would've seriously had to get my eyebrows done for that.

Fuck It Up

Touré Pacquette

LAZARUS: Fuck it up. People want you to take all the bullshit that they put on you. I want to say why the fuck do people put us though all that? We are fucking kids and it feels like they are trying to fuck us up. Like we are not already fucked up. I want to say – maybe I'm wrong – but I'm telling you, fuck it. Feel like when you say something, we are meant to know how we feel at every second of every day… the hell that you put us through and that way we feel.

Just saying – is it even any of your fucking busy how I feel or how other kids feel. No. So fuck off. Stop. Because this shit is going to kill me.

So while I'm still alive I'm going to fuck this shit up, I going to try and make a change so – I know I am swearing a lot but I do not give a fuck. Also, I'm sorry if you're a kid and this is not the same for you and you have your own issues. But I can only speak for me and the kids that feel the same way as I do. The fact is, the world is made for white rich men or middle-class black women or men. But that's just the way the world works. But not enough people question it, not enough people try and change it.

But that's the responsibility of a 13 year kid and all kids worldwide. Do you not see how that is so fucked up? If you don't think about it, think about the amount of shit that you put on us kids. The kids of today are the future of tomorrow. We should look back at the past to make better decisions. The people that came before and try to be better to make a change – that will benefit all of us. But the problems that kids face are one of many pressures that people put on us. We are kids but you don't see that.

I feel trapped, like I can't breathe, like the air in my lungs turned to water. I know I mostly won't win but I just need someone to hear these words to know what is like for me and people like me. I need you to feel the hate I feel around from the second I leave my home to the second I get back.

I'm 13 years old. Tall and black. So people are scared of me without knowing who the fuck I am. So to all those people – fuck you. I'm hated because of the colour of my skin, the way I talk and I'm sick of feeling like shit because of other people's issues. So fuck it up. Fuck it up.

Being A Woman

Ella Ritsema

LUCIE: Do I scare you? Does me being a woman scare you? Probably not. If I were to, say, not shave my leg hairs or my armpits, would that make you uncomfortable? Would you be happier if I had a tiny waist, big bum and big boobs, hairless and careless and free? I'm a woman, silly, I've never been free. Everything we do or say is scrutinised by you. If we speak a word out of line or are a day over thirty or have God forbid *fat* on our bodies, we are erased from society. We don't exist if we aren't a man's idea of a woman. Because men are always right, and we should always do what a man says.

'Oh, I'm a woman, I don't know how to change a lightbulb! But I am expected to carry a child and give birth regardless of whether I want to or not!'

Don't get me wrong, society has changed… to an extent. Women can work and get barely equal pay as men!

'It's a man's world, honey. Don't argue. Just obey.' Obey like a fucking dog am I right? We're your bitches. Does this scare you? A woman swearing. Are you uncomfortable?

'I'm a man and I still have it bad.' Okay, *Joseph*. Do you have it bad when you're walking down a street, alone, at night? Do you have your keys in between your fingers just in case? Just in case a man walks by and does some messed up shit that messes us up for the rest of our lives?! And you'll get away with it.

'But it's not all men, I'm one of the good ones.' I don't care if you're good or bad. We don't know from your face or your pace if you're good or bad. We can't tell. So we back away, protect ourselves. Just in case. Just to be sure. We can never be too sure. We're women. We don't know things. You only want us if we're children. Innocent. Naïve. So you can take advantage of us without batting an eyelid.

Do I scare you? Because you scare me.

I'm Actually Going To Kill Myself

Hannah Morgan

PENELOPE: Fuck I'm hot.

Sorry, that was abrupt.

I'm just stood here. Staring at myself in the mirror, turning left and right to admire all my angles.

I'm playing with my hair, tousling it around as I pose. At one point I turn and look over my shoulder at the mirror. My back is smooth and muscled.

I can't stop staring at myself. It's obsessive, I know.

Two steps from the mirror, right on my tiptoes and leaning over the sink, I stare at my face. The freckles on my nose that only appear when I've spent time in the sun, the mole on my cheek, the occasional spot and my eyebrows. The eyebrows. Perfect eyebrows, sharp and clean without any work. I fucking love my eyebrows.

I've been stood in the mirror for – what? half an hour now? I don't want to exaggerate. Half an hour doesn't seem that long or impressive. But it is a very long time. And it is much longer than I currently have. I should've finished my shower ages ago, and started working as I'd promised, but I'm stood in this stupid mirror enamoured with my own reflection.

And what a reflection it is.

It's not always like this. Sometimes I hate myself. I think I'm ugly and unlovable. So I try to cherish these kinds of moments when I have them.

Moments where I'm spotted in the reflection of a shop window… or a car door. Or those photos that people take of you when you're not looking. Where you look absolutely stunning.

Yes, yes. Call me obnoxious. Call me egotistical. Narcissistic. Conceited. I don't care. I'm fucking hot. Deal with it.

So many times I can't even stand to look in that mirror, so fuck me if I want to once in a while.

Okay. So, I do… sometimes… worry about this obsession.

Sometimes I even think I can't love. That I'll never look at someone the way I look at myself. Or that someone will look at me in the same way.

That sounds so dumb.

My love – just… seems fickle, skin deep. Only it's my own skin. I crave love. For someone to stare at me. Fantasise about me. Obsess over me. Go absolutely fucking insane, thinking about me.

But, well… I suppose that's not love. It sounds rather crazy, actually.

I just want someone to love me as intensely as I love myself.

Perhaps I'll just settle for staring lovingly into my own eyes. Knowing I'll never desire to look into any others.

I'm hot.

Just let me have that.

My Dad

Grace Ford

GRACE: I can hear my dad driving down the path. Gosh he's nearly home! The stones under the tyres scraping as the wheels roll past. It's like they are all running away trying to escape. Do they know too? My little sister's squealing like an underfed pig so excited that he's home. Here we go again. I can hear my dad's Mercedes radio bass banging through the house it's so loud. It's so loud. It's SOO loud! The walls shake. The walls know.

The smell of cheap tobacco climbs its way through the open windows of my bedroom. The dog, oh the dog won't stop running up and down, up and down the creaky stairs. There she is, Mother stands still on the landing as if she's frozen in time. Her face is pale as if she's seen a ghost. You can see the smile has abandoned her face. I hear the clock in my bedroom ticking. It doesn't stop, tick, tick, tick. The car comes to a stop. I look out the window as My Dad steps out. My sister calls out "Daddy, Daddy!" So happy that he's home.

If only she knew what mum and I knew. If only she knew! I run to Mother and take her hand. I look up as a tear rolls down her rosey cheek. She lets out a smile. For a second we forget. For a few moments we forget, then hear the key as it's stabbed into the lock and turns. My Dad. My Dad is home.

Imagine

Jack

EZEKIEL: Imagine you own the only set of keys for a house. They unlock the front door and you're safe. There's no other way to get in and if you lose them everyone knows that you lost them.

Now imagine those keys are your overall HIV status and a main aspect of that is your friends and family's opinion, your own self-perception and your medical records - your deepest fear.

11 years.

Now imagine 11 years of no guidance on how to keep them well or who to tell and being wary of whose hands they could've fallen into.

That was me and so many others that you can't see.

A constant secret and always a lie contradicting even what I believe. And that's just what it's like going to school with the set of keys called HIV.

There Is A Fire

Spike Winstanley

THOMAS: Hello? Can you help? There's a fire.

Hello? Please help. I can t put it out. I can't.

Hello? I need you. Help me. It's on fire. Please.

My house. It's just here, come on. Quick, hurry. I don't know how long we have. It's burning. It's all on fire.

I don't know how it started. Well I sort of do. It wasn't my fault though. I don't think it was.

I've tried putting it out by myself but I can't. I need help. Can you help?

It's getting warmer. Can you feel that? It's getting hotter and hotter and hotter. Why won't it stop? I've tried. I've tried to make it stop.

The flames are growing higher. Don't you see? Why don't you help? Help me please. We need more people. Why won't it stop?

Don't do that. What are you doing? You're not helping. Stop! Stop it. It's larger now. The flames are higher. It's hotter. Hotter, hotter, hotter. What are you doing? The fire is growing. Look what you've done!

I can't stop this. This isn t my fault. I've tried. My house is on fire. You're setting my house on fire.

But it's not just my house. It's yours too! You are setting our houses on fire! All of our houses are burning! Stop it!

The fire engulfs our homes. It won't stop. They are smothered by the flames, collapsing in on one another in defeat. And it's not just our houses. The park is also alight. The trees and the grass and the bushes and the birds burn to the ground. And the sea. The ocean. It catches fire and burns endlessly. I cannot stop it. It fills our lungs and muffles our words. It chokes us. Our skin is burning.

Everything is on fire. The world, in flames. The planet grows hotter. The planet is burning. Our house is burning.

Can you help? There is a fire.

To Be Normal

Rosan Trisic

L: The people in the therapy groups I've been going to - they all describe some sort of primal urge, that they suddenly knew they had to live, to survive. Just as they started to lose feeling in their fingers or just as the rope blocked off their breathing, they'd realise that, deep down, they'd always been reaching out for a hand.

And… I wish I could relate. But I… didn't have that. I just woke up. And I feel guilty for not feeling like that. I feel like I'm just going through the motions of getting better. I feel guilty for my friends who I'm just letting down. I don't know if I don't remember, if something's wrong with me, or if suicide is so rife in the LGBTQ community I barely bat an eyelid at it anymore. I have had three friends attempt suicide in my life. One succeeded. Maybe we're just broken. It can't be a coincidence that about half of all trans youth attempt suicide.

Even so, I feel guilty for not fitting the storyline for 'depressed kid finally appreciates life after suicide'. I feel guilty that I'm not one of those people who will stand up and speak, who will fight on the street and in the courtroom for my brothers, sisters and siblings. I feel guilty that I just want to have a normal life. To be normal.

In real life, the story is never over, for any one. I know people who have been on hormone treatment for years, had the full shebang and they still get abuse lining up in their socials. So much as a 'Hi, I'm transgender' can summon an army of angry profiles.

When I found the LGBTQ+ community, I felt saved. On this pedestal of support I wanted to shout into the universe that I had found myself, finally! Flamboyant Pride protests and spitting at police officers can hide a lot.

So I was pretty surprised when I got kicked out. My parents were supposed to be the ones who were right about everything. But they were also supposed to want the best for me. They took a drill to my skull and made it known, a permanent hole, that I could never be happy if I chose this path. That I could never be normal again.

I didn't know what I was doing, I didn't know where to go. All I had to hold on to was my gut feeling, was the pain that I felt, because it was telling me that I was right. Even when the whole world was screaming at me that I was wrong, that I was confused, that I should be ashamed ...the only thing I had... was the searing pain in my chest and the looming feeling of dread as I looked in the mirror telling me that something was terribly, terribly wrong. And that I needed to be free from it.

But if this is what freedom feels like, then it's shit.

Out Of Sight

Iona Mandal

ANONYMOUS: 'If the world was blind, how beautiful would you be?'
My mind can't help but delve into this thought as I sit on a gently
oscillating park swing this beautiful summer day. A crisp breeze
cools my cheeks, the sun playing hide and seek. I'm not alone. I hear
children giggle, mum's gossip, teens strut across the grass, surprisingly
hushed, enmeshed inside the sticky web of overpowering social
media, their phone screens window to a parallel universe where
online persona is increasingly more important than real self.

I spent last weekend with a close friend listening to podcasts and
baking. But every few minutes, notification 'beep', was commonplace.
Not that I did mind. But is documenting each moment of one's
feelings and experiences for the world so important for 'comments'
and 'likes', as if, providing self-validation, really needed?

Teenagers like me are perpetually caught up in the thought of 'what
will others think' rather than standing to represent their real beautiful
self. My friend loves makeup and fashion. She adjusts her phone and
helps me position to take photographs to be posted online. She asks
me knowing I'll not do a great job anyway! Photography hasn't been
my forte, never will.

Expressing oneself through fashion and makeup is not wrong. True,
a fine line exists between objectifying women with makeup and
making them feel empowered by it. I also ask, how often we have
preconceived notions of someone purely based on looks, not through
their words and actions? How I wish people used their two ears as
much as their eyes for they are equally important!

Is makeup 'forced' on girls constantly under pressure to hide behind
its façade, fearing to show their real self? I don't know if makeup
empowers or hides my friend. My sister helps with the minimal
makeup I wear to look presentable. Like photography, makeup isn't
my skill! Whether creams and powders empower or hide me; make
me strong to peel off my 'second' skin, I'll never know.

It also makes me question, if this second skin resolves or bring in more problems and prejudice? Doesn't it breed unhappiness and isolation for those not fitting established standards of 'accepted' social conformity and 'attractiveness', with low self-esteem and hyper-critical looks, in pursuit of an illusion of 'perfection'? Hasn't it led to constant gazes at the distorted mirror, zooming flaws and even triggering self-harm for the waist is wrong size, skin a wrong colour and lips the wrong shape?

The other day, my friend 'saw' herself on an app, leaving her in tears. After all, she is just a 'normal' teenager experiencing pressures like anyone else! It seems to me that everything must be defined against a strict standard, judged by how we seem and not what we are. But I must admit, I've never seen myself in a mirror for that matter. For I'm a girl, a girl who just happens to be blind.

So, I ask again, 'If the world was blind, how beautiful would you be?'

The Mighty Cough

Maya Choudhury

LAVINA: The power of one cough spread like wildfire. My thoughts are crammed inside this tiny body and I can't let it out. We are trapped. Trapped in this house only allowed out once a day. The vacillating government continues to confuse us.

But there's a tiny spark that glows in our heart. That it will end and all be the same again. That spark is like nothing else, it brings so much joy and love and warms your heart. It's like a bright flame on a candle that will never go out.

Stop listening to that loud dark silence and press that unmute button. That one cough is little yet so ruthless. It hurts us mentally and physically. Don't ignore and pretend to be happy. You need to drown in your sorrows to be able to swim back to the top of the ocean. To take that breath, to pull yourself out of the water, dry those eyes.

When the sorrowness of the world overcomes you. Remember that little spark of hope, even if it's not shown. When the masses of people breathed their last, the reactions weren't full of hatred. They were full of care and worries that brought us together. This is a passage not a place to stay.

What's Going On?

Olivia McGeachy

BEA: Wake up. Please. I don't, I really don't, understand what you're doing. What everybody's doing. With themselves. Y'know? All caught up about what universities to apply to, what phone to buy, what future plans. What future? What plans?

Is that it? Is that what the problem is here? You've not got any future plans? At least, you're pretending not to have any because you're scared of admitting what they are, what they could be, of what you hope to do, of admitting you're not really cut out for being, of doing, anything other than, let me finish, anything other… than making art. Being an artist. Can I ask you something?

What future do any of us have, hope to have, when all we're doing is repressing, and as a result depressing, ourselves - destroying each other, the planet, everything? This whole being alive malarkey. It's painful, sometimes, it can be, can feel, really… awful, y'know. But it's also joyful. Beautiful. Make the most of it.

I know you're trying the best you can, really, the absolute best you can, but come on. Give me a break. Tell me what's wrong, really, actually. Because it's sure as fuck not choosing what university to apply to.

Don't Blame Me

Stella Whitehouse

ELLA: It happened when I was young. I was new to online chat rooms and I was only on them because…well…

I was eleven with no real friends and was the social outcast of secondary school society. The classic quiet bullied kid. I would just chat, I guess, to these strangers. I used a fake name because at least I had one active brain cell working at the time. One day, one of these people asked to chat on some app and I just kinda…agreed. I'm not sure why. Maybe I was bored, maybe I was lonely, maybe it was my bad luck but we exchanged details and continued talking.

It was fine…at first.

He would tell me I was beautiful, that I was sweet and such a good person. It was like… he knew about every piece of human decency I've been deprived of and he spoke it so easily, so sincerely that I thought I finally found someone who saw that I was worth something.

But that… wasn't the case.

He told me to send some…inappropriate pictures.

I was a kid. A sad, lonely kid who was desperate enough that I… agreed because it was what he wanted. He made it sound so normal…about what he was doing, like everyone did this and that he, a fully grown-ass man, could ask that of me.

But after that… he started getting… mean. I kept saying I didn't want to send more, he had enough, why, WHY, would he need more? 'Send me more or all of these photos end up on the internet.'

I was terrified.

Told my mom who then called the police.

The police couldn't do anything. My parents said that they were so disgusted that they couldn't look at my face. Not a single adult cared enough to ask me how I felt. Teachers told us how children must be stupid to do those things, other victims said it ruined their life one way or another.

My therapist said that this childhood trauma was what triggered my depression… and the long list of other mental health issues. I lived every day in fear of those pictures…they appeared in nightmares or crept into my head with the smallest trigger, like eye contact with a stranger on the street. I had anxiety attacks every time I was on the internet, sometimes just by being on Google.

I don't understand how others could treat me… treat my abuse, treat my trauma like it was all my fault.

'How was it abuse if it was online?'

'It was an obvious red flag.'

'You should have said 'no' more.'

'That's what you get for sending those pictures'

It has taken seven years…for me to realise that I shouldn't blame myself. Grooming is abuse, online or offline. I was a child. Does a child deserve this? Why do people shame children for how someone else hurt them? Why do they act like we asked for this?

I didn't ask for this! Don't blame me!

Why My Parents?

Sharmin Jahan

J: 'I'm gonna be late again, ugh.' My hijab wouldn't sit right on my head, my makeup wasn't going on properly, it felt like the whole world's put a curse on me. Having to wear baggy clothes because it was 'modest' or having to cover my ankles or neck cos it was showing too much 'skin', having to come home early because you're a girl, not being able to hang out with the opposite gender because it made me seem like I wanted attention from them, it was so hard being a Muslim girl. Why couldn't my family be like others?

Why couldn't they be less strict or trust me more? I wanna be like the other girls, how they show off their new hair, their new clothes. My parents always think I'm trying to impress someone but the only person I'm trying to impress is me. Make myself feel better, more comfortable, in my own skin. I'm tired of being told my skirt is too long and ugly by my white peers or being told that my skirt was too short and revealing by my brown parents.

Why couldn't my parents be normal for once?

My Little Monster

Freyja Pearman

THE STUDENT: I never thought that living with my monster was going to be easy. I'm stressed, I'm tired, I'm so goddamn tired, and I can't get rid of it. I never expected it to get so big. My manageable little monster is growing so big that I can't see over its head when it sits on my chest and keeps me in bed.

Perhaps I'm being irrational, perhaps I've had my monster so long that the increasingly sinking weight of it on my stomach feels natural. But I cannot ignore the fact that I have a monstrous problem with the monster I have.

It sits on my shoulder, it makes me shake and shudder and I want to hide away because my monster is horrid to look at – and I can't get rid of it. When I try to talk it twists my throat and shoves it down into my stomach and tells me that what I have to say is not worth listening to – and I can't get rid of it. It tells me to work harder, to work less, to go see friends, to hide yourself, it wants to pull me apart in all directions so it can eat what's left – and I can't get rid of it.

Then the panic sets in.

And that's me done for the day. Or week. Or whenever it decides to let go.

The monster has won and I have lost. I try not to keep a tally, but it does. My little monster has grown horns and hair and teeth and a booming voice. And I can't get rid of it. If only I didn't feed it so much. If only I hadn't fed it the majority of my thoughts. But how do you not feed something that's been with you so long it feels like a friend? It's growing all the time but it's still the same little monster – and I can't get rid of it.

We all have monsters. Some people are just finding out about them. Some people have multiple. Some people are still learning to clean up after them. Some people have had their monsters for so long that it's effortless in the way they deal with them. Some people have had their monsters for so long and are still affected by them.

The truth is that you can't get rid of the monster, but you can deal with it.

They're overwhelming and huge and some days just swallow you whole. But you are in control! No matter how big it is, no matter how many fangs or wings or claws or teeth. No matter how much it throws its weight around and screams for attention. You are in control.

We can't get rid of monsters. But we can stop feeding them. We can face them a little more every day. We can choose to not get comfortable with how the monsters treat us; but get comfortable with their presence.

Our little monsters can grow, but we can too!

Green

Maya Hicklin

EDEN: Green. I want to paint my bedroom walls green.

Not neon green or anything, just a nice shade of green. I read one time that it's meant to help you sleep better. I'd imagine there'd be big windows too, with shiny gold hinges. Funky chairs and dressing tables. Littered with trinkets and tokens all completely out of place, yet perfectly positioned. Red brick sounds nice, traditional. Classic. That's how I would want it. Well, how I would have imagined it.

But I'll now be thirty before I can even afford the green paint to lacquer the walls. I might however be able to cop a funky dresser or two but the drawers will remain empty, and if all continues, I'll only have a box full of random bits and bobs, that I have hoarded over the years.

Because why should the next generation be given the opportunity? The opportunity to take their first step on that ladder that you keep dragging further away every time we try to rest our feet upon it! Working hard, setting up saving accounts, budgeting, doing everything we can to be able to form some kind of deposit, to be able to own something. But there's no support, no housing, no chance. Not when the cost of living is valued higher than the price of support.

It works for you though. Always taking. Us giving and giving. Paying rent that we may as well be getting mortgages out for, but never owning. So by all means, keep selling off the affordable housing. We wouldn't want to own anything more than a cardboard box full of tat and a sample-size tin of fawn-green paint.

A Garden In The Belly Of The Beast

Hannah Gbadamosi

HARVEY: I remember this one day, when my mother put a seed on my tongue and told me to swallow. She told me something beautiful would appear to distract others from my sharp, sour tongue.

My tears watered the flower and my red-hot anger, an artificial sun.

And so it grew, grew, grew.

There reached a point when my body could no longer contain what was growing inside me. And so…

The vines shot up.

Up.

Up.

The thorns scratched my insides.

The flower used its claws to attack my throat and as I bled, petals that were previously white, were tainted and stained by my colour red instead.

The flower was waging a war on me, forcing its way from the pit of my stomach into my mouth and bursting out from my lips.

Till it was on display.

People made sure I knew it; telling me how beautiful, how lovely it was.

They saw me choking on the flower's head.

They saw me choking and told me how beautiful, how lovely it was.

Suffocating. Suffering.

Too much to bear.

Too painful.

I kept cutting at the flower's thick neck hoping. Praying that I could separate myself from this beautiful curse so that I might be able to take a breath without being hit by the stench of roses.

Clawing.

Clawing until its head fell off.

Clawing until I exposed what was lying behind the closed doors that were my lips: ugly scars, twisted vines that had made a home inside of me and bloody thorns.

I had nothing left to disguise my sour words with anymore.

But what was a little vinegar dripping from my lips if it meant I didn't have to deal with thorns anymore? What was a little lemon juice on my tongue if I could breathe again?

Imperfect Reflections

Matilda Lucas

JESSIE: Is this alright?… a bit short, isn't it?… No, it is… I'll change, I'll just change…

Me? Oh, I'm fine… fine really… Do I look OK in this?… Lucy doesn't think she looks OK at the moment… I'm worried about Lucy… I just wonder what she sees when she looks in the mirror… she says she doesn't like herself at the moment… and mum, I think she might be sick… I don't know if she's OK… she's so thin, mum and… she's always wearing long jumpers and baggy T-shirts… I think she might be trying to hide something…

She's definitely eating differently as well… she only picks at her food at lunch and has stopped having a snack at breaktime… she's still doing her netball though… if anything she seems to be doing more than usual… what do you think I should do? I want to help her, but I don't want to get her in trouble … I just think looking at all those Instagram posts isn't good for any of us… It just makes me so angry… all the filters and posing it's just not real… it puts so much pressure on us all… trying to be like them… it's just not good for us … it's not good for Lucy … it's all so unhelpful… and she needs help…

Why do people stop eating mum? Is it just so they look good or is it something deeper? Are they unhappy mum? So, I think the Adidas leggings are better than the jeans… but my thighs do look quite big in these…

You Made A Joke

Mia Beckmann Adams

FEMINA: You made a joke. A joke about safe streets.

I wiped a tear from the eye of my friend who had walked on them, the real streets, the streets of the country your people dictate.

Perhaps I don't care about you spending your figures, or naming numbers and initiatives that never happen. Perhaps I didn't go to the police, for what if I was greeted by a 'wrongen' or one of those few 'bad apples' – the kind of fruits that laugh about crimes they don't prosecute.

I heard your joke. And I didn't laugh. I didn't cry or shout either. For your mind is too clouded with the smoke of another world, whose aliens won't understand a reality that isn't theirs.

You lost your place and made a joke about the impossible opposite to catcalls, stares, harassment, disappearances, kidnap, murder, rape. When I lose my place I say 'I lost my place' and silently berate myself for giving them a chance to look away from my face.

Somehow no words of mine will make an impact. I am not asking for an advance solely by your hand. So do not quote your stats at me. I ask for jokes about things that are funny and something called 'taking things seriously'.

I know, I ask in vain. Your green seats are impermeable. Life's gravel too ingrained for even someone who cared… to really change.

Pan With Pride

Frederick Hall

MARCUS JOHNSON: I struggled for a long time to find the right words to say to you both – Mum do you remember that time in prep school when we did that gender swapped play and I had to dress up in a dress and put on all that make-up? I fought against it so hard but when it was on suddenly I didn't want to take it off, it was like this part of me had been awoken and since then it has never gone back to sleep.

Dad, remember when we went to that swimming pool and you told me off for staring at the woman there and I was so confused? Well that's because it wasn't the woman I was staring at. I struggled for so long to find the words to truly summarise who I was. But my sister, you will remember that secret that you kept for me and I am so grateful to you for not telling everyone about my girlfriend…

And the truth is I did love her until she finally realised what everyone eventually realised… that I don't know who I am.

I spent ages locked away in my room pushing you out of my life, experimenting with my body the way every teen boy does but something always felt incompetent, like I was staring at my life through a keyhole unable to open the door. This was when I realised - I loved girls but I also love boys. I didn't care which gender they associated themselves with, I loved people as people… but I didn't know or understand what this meant until I went to Pride and like that, it all slipped into place.

I wasn't gay, I wasn't straight, and most importantly, I wasn't broken. I was pan. And I'm pan with pride.

Unspeakable

Izzie Dickinson

V: My head has been a dangerous place ever since you died. A place not even the most criminal of criminals deserves to be sent to. A place not even the richest person on earth could buy their way out of. Although if they could, I would give all my money just to escape the chains trapping me in my mind, just for the afternoon. When I close my eyes each night, a red blur filters my dreams. I try to wake myself up, pull myself up out from the increasing feeling of drowning, but I can't. I'm sinking too fast. I wake up in the night, gasping for breath but all around me are the people in my dreams, only more real. Walking towards me, whispering words I can't understand, yet am so afraid of.

I suppose in a way, my mind has always been like this. Unforgiving. But you had your ways of giving me somewhere else to go. When I was with you, it was as if my mind forgot its job of making my life miserable, and instead got lulled by your sweet voice, just as I had. My mind is a ditch that I had been stuck in for many years, and you built me a ladder, so I could get out. Something so simple, yet something nobody had ever though to do for me. Or maybe they have, and simply couldn't be bothered.

Yet that ladder broke when you died, along with my heart, it shattered into pieces, and I myself am not mentally strong enough to put them back together, in fact I fear I never will be. My own head is swallowing me up inside, eating away at me, talking to me like I am nothing and it is everything, though in my every day life, it is. My mind is my daytime and my nighttime. It is the backing music to my study and shouts loudly when I speak, drowning out my voice in the world, so that eventually I go mute altogether.

I tell myself nobody deserves this, that it will get better, that I need to push to stay strong, though I guess my own mind was the punishment I had been warned about. As I stare at your dead body strapped to the wall with duct tape, one thought in my mind speaks louder than the rest. Why did they make me do this to you?

Trapped

Maryam

URSUS: HEY, MR ZOOKEEPER! Don't you know this is not my home. Everywhere I turn I can see faces and there is too much noise! MY home was silent. My fur is hot and wet… care to brush it? No, didn't think so. What are you doing with that bucket? You are tipping my food into the lake. Do you have no respect for me? Or are you trying to start a show? How about I take that cup you're holding and smash it with my sharp claws? What are you trying to achieve?

Those strange human faces couldn't care less whether I am alive or dead. The money donations they give you! Try using them on me, not to fund your missions to take more of my type from the icy Tundra. Tell them to stop cheering. I will not put a show on for you sir. NO. N.O. Having trouble understanding my language? Maybe If you had learned it in the first place, I would not be here.

I am not going to move; I can hear you telling your big fat lies to your audience of faces. Telling them about my kind. How about you tell them I'm a polar bear with no choice? 'The UK is a perfect habitat for these animals.' You, sir, are an animal with no respect, and I think you should go away and leave us alone! Because clearly you just aren't happy with the wildlife in your country. GO AWAY. LEAVE. Before I make friends with the wildlife, and then you'll be sorry because we will push you out and you will have nowhere else to go.

I could easily walk over to the lions in the cage opposite and unlock it. WE would be the perfect team, us lions and bears. What is that smirk on your face? I see, you still don't understand. We both have very sharp teeth, sharp claws and a newly found appetite. So, I think I'll pass on breakfast today, considering there could be a banquet waiting straight for me. How does that sound? MR ZOOKEEPER.

Minority Identity

Rianna Kumar

In her history class **ALICIA** *sits at her desk reluctantly putting her hand up to answer a question. She watches her peer answer instead.* **ALICIA** *shows signs of frustration with her peer's answer.*

ALICIA: You sit up there, on your throne. With your perfectly pointed nose and your bright blue eyes and yet you still refuse to see. You speak like this was a choice for me, like I chose to be the odd one out here. 'It's okay Alicia, I can't be racist! My dog walker's half-cousin's-sister is half black.' Or my personal favourite, 'it's okay Alicia, I can't be racist because I don't see race.' That's the problem. Can't you see?

You claim to hear us, with your performative reposts every so often on 'how to make life easier for people of colour' on your story, like we're some sort of outcasts who don't live and breathe the same as you. And those petitions you always link in your bio, knowing fine well nobody gives two shits about them. But do you listen? Do you listen to the cries of my ancestors at the hands of yours? The bloodshed? The agony? The genocide of my people, at the hands of the man you just claimed to be a 'war hero'?

Oh, forgive me! Am I making you uncomfortable? I tell myself, 'There's no point Alicia' in trying to educate those who refuse to unlearn what they already think they know. It sounds crazy, but I think I would much rather be called a 'darkie bitch' to my face than put up with your performative bullshit. Because for you, being accused of racism is just as horrific as being the victim of it. It's like screaming at the top of your lungs. Until you shred every single vocal cord in your throat. But you're doing it at a ten-foot white wall. I don't want your pity. I don't want your white tears. I want acceptance.

Homework

Malena Clarke-Fogg

MADISON: Square root of 361. What is this? What even is a square root? OK, skip it. I'll come back to it. Volume of a cylinder. Volume of a cylinder. A cylinder doesn't make noise! Have we learnt about this? God, my brain cells hurt. This is so dull. How am I supposed to help sleeping in maths if all we're learning about is this?

Her phone rings.

Hi! Jackie!

Wait, the party's tomorrow?

No, I didn't forget! I lost track of time!

No they are not the same thing.

Look I got homework to do see you later.

Bye!

Square root of 361. Square numbers. We did this in primary. A number times by itself and one? No, that's prime. Square is… ITSELF TIMES BY ITSELF! Got it! So now what do I do?

Her phone buzzes.

Oh my God what do they want now? Ew what is that? Oh, the before and after of Jackie's dog Doggy salon day! Reply: 'Aw how cute! Hearteyes, hearteyes, hearteyes.' Send.

OK cylindrical volume.

She pauses.

OK, MUM, GOT IT! Ten minutes until dinner. I can finish this by then. Positive vibes.

Her phone rings again.

Hi Jackie! Why are you calling?

(Quietly.) Again.

Yes. Dress code. I know.

Ew pink? No, I wasn't going to wear pink!

You saw the picture.

That was for something else, a…wedding I'm…going to…on…Saturday.

I need to go, Homework.

Your dog is adorable by the way.

Hangs up.

(Screaming.) LEAVE ME ALONE!

YES MUM, I'M FINE!

Livin' my best live with the square root of a cylinder. Or the volume. Whatever.

I need to find a new dress.

Looks around for a bit.

OK, this one will do. Bonus: It isn't pink.

Maths. OK, I can't do this. Estimation time!

123 grams. This is fine. Extra question. People who must complete are Abby, Ryan, Jackie, Madison. WHY? WHY ME?

FIVE MINUTES MUM I KNOW!

20 people are on a subway. There are 18 seats in the carriage. On the next three stops, seven people leave, and an additional 34 get on. How many people are standing? HOW SHOULD I KNOW? Why can't the flipping passengers work it out? Who needs to know?

WHAT DOES SHE WANT NOW?

(Falsetto.) Do you like my dress? It's gold and sparkly. I can see that. Reply: OMG you look great!

20-7. 13. 13+34= What's the ANSWER?

Her phone rings.

Leave me alone!

I'M BUSY!

Hangs up.

Yes Mum, I'm coming.

13+34. 3+4=7, 1+3=4, 44. 44-18 – YES, MUM, I AM COMING! 8 minus 4 doesn't go. So carry the 10, 8-14 – GIVE ME A MINUTE! – equals 6, 3-1=2, 26. Twenty– NEARLY THERE! – Six. SUBMIT!

I'M DONE!

YES, MUM, I'M COMING!

It's Not Enough

Nathan Mitchell

NANCY: It's not enough. It's not enough. Law? Law? Doesn't do enough. I can't take it, it's like… Why? Why? It's not enough.

Nothing.

I get… looks. Looks. Why? Why? I can't… it's not enough. Where's the charge. Who's… in charge? I can't tell who I am. Not… not anymore. It's a burning. A burning. What does it even mean? To be me? Don't know. Not anymore. I'm broken.

Am I broken? They think so, they think so. Think I'm wrong, unnatural. Broken. I can't… it's not enough, it's not enough. No-one does enough. Do I do enough? Or is being enough? Monsters.

They call us… monsters. It's not enough. It's a burning – not enough. I'm not a monster, just me. Just me. Just… why? Insides are fractured and I can't be enough. Enough woman, enough man, enough anything. I want to be enough woman, enough man, enough… They hate me. They…

It's not enough. I want to be enough woman, and no man. I… Am. Broken. Don't wanna die a boy. Don't wanna. Don't wanna grow as a man. I'm a monster. I'm a monster. I'm a – not enough. Not enough. Don't do enough. No help. No support. They don't care. They hate me. It's – stigma. I can't grow old, I can't. Can't… kids. Not mine, never mine. Can't be mine. Can't be mine. Can't be mine. Can't be mine. Forced one way or another. Me. Parts are you. Parts are… gross.

Between your legs, you. It's not… Me. Not me. Mine aren't me. Not right. It's not enough. Don't wanna die a boy. Don't wanna die a boy. Don't… don't tell me. Don't tell me if… Don't tell me if you think I'm unnatural. I'm a monster, I'm a monster. I'm.

'S'

Lewis Canning

JAMIE: It seems weird to dislike a letter. A word. I mean, how can you possibly hate what is effectively just a combination of squiggles? How can you get nervous thinking about a squiggle? ... But I do. I hate a letter. I know it's crazy but that single letter makes me feel so lost, so insecure. So alone.

I hate the letter 'S'. But of the 164,777 words with that letter, I only have a problem with one. It seems wrong to condemn a letter for a word that is only 0.000006% of its use. But I do. Hate the letter 'S'.

I used to have parents. Plural. Now I have a parent. Just one.

'S' follows me. I'm constantly reminded that whilst my friends are out eating with their two parents, I am sat at home with only one of mine.

I wish the 'S' was there, I often forget it ever left. But I am dragged into the real world. The real world that simply isn't ready for this case. Look, I won't say that my story is as unique as 1 in 164,777 – it's certainly an outlier.

Even typing out this message, there is a blue line under the word 'parent' – telling me to 'check my grammar', but unfortunately, cancer doesn't listen to edit suggestions. How am I supposed to come to terms with this if even Grammarly is telling me it's wrong? I know it's wrong. But it's true. The world isn't ready for this story, and I don't think I am either.

Loneliness

Genevieve Wolff

ISABELLE: They say loneliness is the greatest comfort.

Well I see no beauty in being alone.

The absent noise of chatter and laughter is the loudest reminder that I am not there. And as I sit upon my bed, engrossing myself in the abstract fantasies of what I dream my life to have been, I cannot help but wonder how my desired reality is one so far from this. It pains me to think I will never truly be at peace knowing I do not wish to be here.

Night after night, day after day, I piece together fragments of my imagination, creating metaphysical worlds in hopes to find a source of comfort within me. I suppose it works for a while; a temporary escape. But for now I sit here alone, along with a heart filled with discontent. And the fleeting shadow of reality lying just beneath my grasp.

I will never understand how emptiness can feel so heavy, but maybe one day I'll learn to be at peace with this burden. This weight. Maybe one day I'll learn to be, feel, content with this loneliness. I'll sit in coffee shops and watch strangers converse. I'll imagine their lives, their feelings, their secrets.

And as night falls, I'll bathe in the essence of my fantasies. I'll dream of flying through the clouds on gossamer wings. I'll dream of diving into the deep blue sea. I'll dream of walking into a world unknown, and I'll dream of castles so tall you cannot see the peak.

Because in dreams, I am in control and what I wish to be, will be. And though I know it is not real, it's often better than reality.

Yes… as dawn rises, my dreams shall end, but I'll wait. I know that the train of my subconscious will be there at dusk. I suppose that's what keeps me going; the reliance upon my imagination.

So… I'll learn to be lonely.

I'll learn to let the absence of noise comfort me, and I'll learn to see my worlds as amusements and not as escapes.

I'll learn to see the beauty…

In being alone.

Bunker At War

Pearce Donachy

A Ukrainian bunker. **JOSEPH** *is playing a game of chess.*

JOSEPH: It started just a fortnight ago. I was sleeping, more, more tired than ever after a football match.

How did it come to this? My life ruined. Destroyed by a power hungry… The only thing keeping me from total boredom was my liking of chess. I would play for hours with other victims of this horrific event.

Moving pawns. It was like my life was a game of chess being taken by the other teams' pawn and thrown away, off the chess board, never to be seen again.

The bunker was the only thing between me and death from missile strikes, which were common every day. Every night I would be woken by BOOM! BANG! SMACK! And then hearing the endless screaming from other people living in the bunker.

One morning I was greeted by my father - 'how was your day?'

I replied with – 'another depressing day of living in a bunker.'

The next things he said to me had me in shock – 'well, we're leaving.'

I stood in amazement. 'But sadly it comes with repercussions,' he said.

Suddenly my face went from smiling for the first time in a while, then fell back to sadness like every day.

'I'm going to have to stay and fight,' my father said in a sad tone. I didn't what to be sad or happy or mad, I had two days left with my dad. We sat and played chess for hours at a time until those two days were up. I said farewell and left alone with another two people driving to the border.

Where Are You From?

Stephanie Oluwatamilore Abogunrin

TÁDÉSE: 'What are you?' What? 'What are you?' Pardon? 'Where are you from?' Ireland? 'No, where are you really from?

I'm Irish. I'm Irish. I'm Irish, I say, with my brown skin, my wide lips, my afro hair. And after I say this, I see their reaction. Their frustration. Their confusion. Their inability to understand.

And so, I continue, but my family is from. My family is from. My family is from. But that wasn't the question. The question was where I come from. Where I really come from. And to be honest, I don't know. I didn't lie. I am a child of the Emerald Isle, conceived and born here, raised in the North, frequently visiting the South. All I've ever known is here. My family, my friends, my foundations. And yet, there's a part of me that feels like I'm lying.

When I look in the mirror, I don't see a child of Ireland. I don't see the pale skin, the ginger hair, the bright eyes. I see an outsider.

And when I walk the streets, I don't see family and friends. I don't see welcoming eyes or encouraging smiles. I see fearful people.

And when I look at the flag, the glorious tricolour, I don't see my foundations, or feel a sense of belonging. I don't feel unity, or inclusion, or hope. Instead, I see green and orange, united by white in their condemnation of Black. In their condemnation of me.

Because when they ask you what you are, where you're from, where you're really from, they already have an answer. You're an immigrant, a 'Black', from somewhere that isn't here. And you're not allowed to forget it. And I don't.

Because if I say I'm not Irish, then I'm ungrateful. Ungrateful for the life I've led, the opportunities I've had, the home that's mine. And if I say I am, then I've condemned my roots, my heritage, my forefathers and their sacrifices.

But why? Why must I condemn one to embrace the other? Why can't I choose my identity? Maybe because I've never been allowed to. Maybe because others have always chosen it for me. And I have accepted their choice. Accepted their choice and crafted my own answer. An answer that indicates that I am not fully Irish or fully daughter of immigrants.

But why can't I fully be both? I am both. My home and my heritage are intertwined, equal parts of my identity. No Blacks, no dogs, no Irish. I am Black, and I am Irish. There is no shame in that. No fine print. No missing detail.

I am human, I am from Ireland, and I am Black.

Mr Speaker

Leila Biggs

MS: Are you fucking kidding me? I'm sorry, Mr Speaker, but I open Instagram this morning and all I see is men posting about sexual harassment awareness. 50% of which I know for a fact have either sexually harassed girls or are still best mates with someone that has. All these performative posts like you actually give a single shit about us. If you didn't care before, you don't care now. And that's the truth of it.

No, I will not change my tone. What is it? Do you feel emasculated? Am I humiliating you? Are you embarrassed? Aw, poor men. Poor you. You're worried us women are going to humiliate you; we're worried you're going to rape and murder us. Get over yourself. I mean seriously, who do you think you are? In the grand scheme of things, you're no one. You're absolutely no one. You think you're everything. You think you're the shit, don't you? Oh yeah, you're the man; you're the lad, the geez, the guy. 'Oi, lad you want to get a pint? Yeah sure geez I'll be there'. FUCK OFF.

I'm sorry, Mr Speaker, but no one cares. No one gives a shit about the fact you like to go to parties and have a good time. Because it's the girls you're groping and and the girls you're calling a psycho bitch and the girls you're calling frigid and the girls you're convincing to fuck you after they said no six times. It's the girls who go home crying when they have to watch you walk around the shop chatting, laughing, fucking fist pumping the boys who will never understand what you've put her through. So shut the actual fuck up about your post of '97% of young women experience sexual harassment'.

WE KNOW. WE KNOW BECAUSE WE HELP MAKE UP THAT PERCENTAGE YOU IDIOT. AND DON'T YOU DARE APOLOGISE TO ME. INSTEAD, APOLOGISE TO THE GIRLS WHO ARE CRYING SO HARD INTO THEIR PILLOWS THEY'VE HAD TO PLAY MUSIC SO THEIR PARENTS DOWNSTAIRS DON'T HEAR.

Thank you.

Strawberry Milk!

Kuhu Agarwal

AMIRA: When I was a little kid, in reception, I was drinking strawberry milk and a girl came up to me and said, 'Hey! Wow, I like the colour of your milk. It's so different!' – that made me the happiest girl ever. Being different made me so happy. Ever since then, all I ever wanted to do was to be different. Be the light in the corner.

I'd say I'd want to be the first girl to fly or the first girl to, you know, eat a thousand cheeseburgers or something else like that. My mum would be like, 'Do whatever you want sweetie, savour your childhood' … I used to get confused about that, what does she mean?

Like why couldn't I savour it when I was older? Until high school, I'd come on dress up day as someone against the theme. As something outrageously funny. Like a, like a Teletubby!

Giggles, then stops abruptly.

I always thought that the other girls in my class were laughing with me rather than at me. So, I would do the same giggle I just did, but then more ecstatic. More joyful. It never once occurred to me they could be laughing *at* me. But back then, I guess I wouldn't have cared.

You see, I've never been the smart one. Sometimes the creative one, but reading people wasn't exactly my strength. Unless someone tells me directly, I'll always just assume they were actually being nice. Like if a girl says, 'I like your shoes. They're so interesting,' no matter how she says it, my first thought will be, she's just kind. And even if they say something unkind directly, it's not like I don't get bothered. I just remember, I'll probably never see them in my life again.

That's one thing high school is good for. It teaches me to literally not care about people's opinions of me. I'm only at high school for like what? 1/10th of my life? That is if I live for 70 years, so I might as well spend it being happy. And for me there really isn't any greater joy than my friends and family, my aspirations and… my most unique. Special. Different from them all. Strawberry milk.

Heath Fire

Marion Memmi Weir

GEN *is sitting on a stump in a landscape that was once a vibrant heath. A week ago, all of it burned in a wildfire. The ground and remaining twigs of vegetation all look disturbingly black, as if someone had drenched the whole scene in ink.*

GEN: I came here a lot in lockdown. In the summer. There was nothing to do – no exams to revise for, no school. Just this – vacuum – of time between then and September.

So I'd come here. I liked it because it was quiet. It was so open, like it went on forever. And, yeah, I know that if you look on Google Earth, bird's eye, it's just a bubble of dusty brown and green circled by houses – the last bit of ground the town hasn't eaten up.

But when you're walking there for the first time, it feels infinite.

Beat.

They say lots of lizards died. I never got to see a lizard. I haven't visited in a while – been too busy revising. Bit fucking rude of me, really.

Beat.

They'll be shaking their fists, saying it was arson. And maybe it was. And then they'll praise the firefighters, which they damn well should. And then we'll all be sad and cry about the lizards, and right after that we'll jump back into our cars and get on with our lives.

We won't talk about why the heath was so dry, so flammable, this time of year.

Beat.

It'll take fifteen years to restore. I won't see it again until I'm thirty-three, and that's if another fire doesn't burn it up before that.

Beat.

I don't know what to do. I can't do nothing, but I know how difficult change is – my politics teachers try to get us to answer questions like

'What is the most effective method of protest?' or 'Where does power really lie?'

And I think I know.

Frustration builds.

If you want change, you can sign petitions, you can go to protests, you can donate to charities – but power is so concentrated at the top, that, if we don't change who sits at the top, they'll write-off our petitions, they'll laugh at our protest, and they'll leave the heavy lifting to charities.

We care. God, we care. We're sad, and angry, and want the world to be a fairer place. We have so much energy – but why aren't we voting? Why do we shy away from politics?

This year, laws have been passed that limit our right to protest, increase police powers, and stop the courts from challenging the government. That fucking scares me – and until the next election, there's nothing we can do about it.

It's easy to switch off. There's so much jargon and infighting, so much white noise. But if we disengage, injustices won't change. Problems will get worse. The ground will get drier. Fires will get bigger and – one day – we won't have enough water to put them out.

What Am I Missing?

Ruby Pegues

RORY PRITCHETT: Ever since the age of six, every adult I've ever met has told me the same thing. 'Wow you're a big talker, you'd be a great politician.'

I think for a while I didn't quite understand what that meant, 'big talker' in my mind meant that I must have a pretty loud voice, which I suppose would be great for talking in front of lots of people? That wasn't quite the case but gradually it started to make sense.

What they really meant was that I was somebody who could ramble on for hours about absolutely nothing and yet somehow manage to make it out to be something, better yet to be something of importance. Which, I soon realised, was the essential skill needed to become a politician.

You no longer have to know what you're doing, you no longer need some elaborate plan. You simply have to know how to pretend like you have everything under control. For such a long time I kept wondering what I was missing.

I would go over every interview, every speech, every television broadcast and even stalk their social media. Just to find something. Surely I am missing something, because as far as I can see there is no method to their madness. Yet, here they are.

We are living in a world that is dying, that is slowly deteriorating day by day and still nobody seems to care enough. We all just turn the other way. Maybe it's because we believe that if we pretend it's not there, it doesn't exist. Maybe it's because we feel that we're only one person so what difference would it make? Or maybe we just don't want to entertain the idea that these people standing up in front of us may not have everything under control after all.

All I know is that if we don't start to wake up and make a change, it's gonna become pretty hard to ignore when we're facing the consequences. That is why I am standing here today, asking you to vote for me. I know I don't have everything under control but I know I am not going to sit around waiting for something to happen before I take action.

Cocoon

Poppy Fair

NARRATOR: It is easy philosophy to make.
    That sick Saturdays are a tragedy,
    More so than another day of the week.
    Confinement to one room in the morning,
    To be so painfully aware of Time
    Dripping leisurely because you can't sleep,
    And then to find that when you were asleep
    It was clutching crumpled kitchen paper;
    Disintegrating skin where the nose curves.
    All cavities in your face actually,
    Feeling busy and dry and overrun,
    Like something heavy and rounded streaming
    On a hard surface – snooker, or marbles.
    I hate the taste of illness in my mouth.

I can hear my phone pulsating somewhere
Hidden in my bed sheets on a groupchat.
It seems to be far away from my skin
As I watch the sun spill through the curtains.
I see a pretty, buttery colour.
A cat lunges up to the windowsill,
Oversat'rated with rich red and grey;
I look at her crookedly from my bed
While she looks back with blank and shining eyes.
She licks her lips slowly, deliberately,
And draws away her stare to slink around,
Sliding with languid light-footedness back
Into the red brick of the alleyway.
Feathery weeds are growing from the walls,
In yellow and in green, they rock gently.
The picture lolls in warmth like it's breathing.

Once the light has drained from the sky there is
An artificial blue film over it,
It's the same colour as blue cellophane.

The groupchat is going to town to walk
Amidst the blue on uneven pavement –
Drink something fizzy and aromatised,
Taste it in your nose instead of your tongue.
I can't taste anything at any rate.
Instead I'm just lying and thinking of
The look of neon lights in front of clubs,
And loud music and silvery taxis.
It's blurry and it melts together lots
But I'm still here making my blanket nest
In bed with suffocating clarity.
I can imagine a lady made up
Of glow sticks and glitter and ID cards,
Beckoning me with a long fingertip,
Just lazily curling and uncurling –
While I sit and, with great regretfulness,
Consider the flavour of my own mouth.

Unrequited

Tara Chetty Audit

ROBIN: I have known her my whole life. It's just been the two of us for as long as I can remember. Born in the same hospital 3 days 4 hours apart. Our mums met at antenatal classes. We like the same movies, like *Paper Towns*, *IT* (my personal favourite), and *The Perks of Being a Wallflower*. Her favourite quote is 'we accept the love we think we deserve' which is from the film. We do everything together. We go to concerts, cry at the same things, laugh at the same things. We actually have a 100% match on Spotify. We are best for each other.

Beat.

I remember at the ripe old age of 9 we were both jamming out to Taylor Swift in my garden, choreographing every step to *Shake It Off* and *Love Story*. When she asked me 'where do you see yourself in 10 years?'

I didn't think much of it then and spoke.

'Probably an astronaut living on Mars…what about you?' She replied, 'I'm not sure yet, but I know for a fact that I'll be with you.'

I knew from that moment she was my forever person.

I think I know her better than anyone else in the whole world. You could practically say that we were siblings. I often find myself thinking about how lucky I am to have her, to be MY best friend.

I can't exactly place the date when my feelings for her shifted from platonic to romantic. I kind of hoped the feelings would die down, but…

The more I think about her and us, the more I want it to be my reality. Maybe I don't want it to go away. Maybe it is here for a reason, for me to…to tell her how I feel.

BUT

Beat.

If I tell her, will she feel the same? Would it be our forever love? Would we fly away into a magical future?

Or…

Beat.

If I tell her, will it be the end?

Will it break our bond? Our sandbox love? Would we even be friends still? I don't want this. I don't want my feelings to be the bane of our relationship. I just want it to be simple. I'm a simple person, I've always been a simple person. I don't want to put her in a position where she feels I have betrayed our friendship for these feelings…of…love.

Will it ruin everything?

If I ignore it, will it only grow stronger? I'm sure it's not unrequited, we're so close it's practically inevitable… so I suppose what's there to lose. Apart from our friendship.

Beat.

You know what, you only live once. I'll never know if I don't go for it. What if I regret not telling her in years to come when we are all grown up and married with kids. I would never forgive myself.

I'm going to build up the courage and I'm going to ask her. Today…

I Just Can't Do It

Lauryn Head

LORI: My executive dysfunction's killing me. I've got homework for tomorrow that I haven't even looked at… and I've been starving since I got home from school, but… now it's midnight and I haven't eaten. I want to do it and it would be so easy to do it. But… I can't. I just… lie here. Scrolling through stuff on my phone that I don't even care about. Or just staring at the ceiling, doing literally nothing except screaming at myself to be productive or something.

And I don't even always know if this is my autism, or if I have any other stuff that I'm just passing off as my autism and not treating, or if it's actually just me being lazy and making excuses for myself. What if I'm just telling myself it's okay because I can't help it, when I can? What if I'm screaming at myself for not doing more, when I genuinely can't? Why can't I just help myself… or talk to others about this so I can get something done for once?

And it's even worse for school. It's getting so much harder to get my work done now. My stimming's worse. I focus so hard on focusing that I forget to focus. Every random thought that pops up into my head is just another rabbit hole and I can't stop falling into them. And that's only when I can focus on one train of thought instead of having sixteen tabs open in my brain and I can't find the one that keeps playing… I dunno… rickrolls, on flipping loop. And then the teachers always call me 'studious' and 'a good listener.' At least my masking's useful.

But I don't care how many times I'm told that I can get a B or… that I can do this or that I just… need a few more marks. I just can't do that, okay? It's getting harder and harder, I'm doing worse on every test, I just can't keep doing it.

It makes me feel like a toddler that needs to be led by the hand all the time and taught about every little thing because 'she doesn't understand yet, but it's not her fault, it's just her development'… but then… I still mess up all the tests and sit there feeling… like a liability every lesson.

I'm the kid that stares dumbly at you for two minutes after you give them the simplest task... and then eventually starts to slowly screw it all up. Not on purpose, I just... didn't process it right or... I didn't understand. And people get so angry about that. They don't want to help... or... if they do, they don't realise I need it. They just remind me that I could do better... that everyone else is doing better... that it doesn't take nearly as long as I make it.

If they don't help, I... wish they'd at least teach. I can't teach myself everything that others just... pick up.

Be Your Own You

Evan Maguire

JACK: Just be yourself. Don't be like anybody else. Be your own you.

Just be yourself. Don't be like anybody else. Be your own you.

Just be yourself. Don't be like anybody else. Be your own you.

Just be yourself. Don't be like anybody else. Be your own you.

Just be yourself. Don't be like anybody else. Be your own you.

Just be yourself. Don't be like anybody else. Be your own you.

Just be yourself. Don't be like anybody else. Be your own you.

Just be yourself. Don't be like anybody else. Be your own you.

Just be yourself. Don't be like anybody else. Be your own you.

Just be yourself. Don't be like anybody else. Be your own you.

Just be yourself. Don't be like anybody else. Be your own you.

Just be yourself. Don't be like anybody else. Be your own you.

Just be yourself. Don't be like anybody else. Be your own you.

Just be yourself. Don't be like anybody else. Be your own you.

Just be yourself. Don't be like anybody else. Be your own you.

Just be yourself. Don't be like anybody else. Be your own you.

Just be yourself. Don't be like anybody else. Be your own you.

Just be yourself. Don't be like anybody else. Be your own you.

Just be yourself. Don't be like anybody else. Be your own you.

Just be yourself. Don't be like anybody else. Be your own you.

Just be yourself. Don't be like anybody else. Be your own you.

Just be yourself. Don't be like anybody else. Be your own you.

Just be yourself. Don't be like anybody else. Be your own you.

Just be yourself. Don't be like anybody else. Be your own you.

Just be yourself. Don't be like anybody else. Be your own you.

Just be yourself. Don't be like anybody else. Be your own you.

Just be yourself. Don't be like anybody else. Be your own you.

Just be yourself. Don't be like anybody else. Be your own you.

Just be yourself. Don't be like anybody else. Be your own you.

Just be yourself. Don't be like anybody else. Be your own you.

Just be yourself. Don't be like anybody else. Be your own you.

Just be yourself. Don't be like anybody else. Be your own you.

Just be yourself. Don't be like anybody else. Be your own you.

Just be yourself. Don't be like anybody else. Be your own you.

Just be yourself. Don't be like anybody else. Be your own you.

Just be yourself. Don't be like anybody else. Be your own you.

Just be yourself. Don't be like anybody else. Be your own you.

Just be yourself. Don't be like anybody else. Be your own you.

Just be yourself. Don't be like anybody else. Be your own you.

Just be yourself. Don't be like anybody else. Be your own you.

Just be yourself. Don't be like anybody else. Be your own you.

Just be yourself. Don't be like anybody else. Be your own you.

Resources

Podcast

To accompany Unmute, LUNG has launched a podcast with professional recordings of all the monologues. To listen, visit feeds.acast.com/public/shows/unmute or wherever you get your podcasts.

Get Support

If you, or someone you know, has been affected by some of the themes in this book, support is available to you.

Childline

Childline is here to help anyone under 19 in the UK with any issue they're going through.

You can talk about anything. Whether it's something big or small, our trained counsellors are here to support you.

Childline is free, confidential and available any time, day or night. You can talk to us:

- by calling 0800 1111
- by visiting www.childline.org.uk

Samaritans

Samaritans works to make sure there's always someone there for anyone who needs someone. Whatever you're going through, call us for free anytime:

- by calling 116 123
- emailing jo@samariants.org
- by visiting www.samaritans.org

Salamander Street